At a Play

Level 6 – Orange

Helpful Hints for Reading at Home

The graphemes (written letters) and phonemes (units of sound) used throughout this series are aligned with Letters and Sounds. This offers a consistent approach to learning, whether reading at home or in the classroom.

HERE IS A LIST OF PHONEMES FOR THIS PHASE OF LEARNING. AN EXAMPLE OF THE PRONUNCIATION CAN BE FOUND IN BRACKETS.

Phase 5			
ay (day)	ou (out)	ie (tie)	ea (eat)
oy (boy)	ir (girl)	ue (blue)	aw (saw)
wh (when)	ph (photo)	ew (new)	oe (toe)
au (Paul)	a_e (make)	e_e (these)	i_e (like)
o_e (home)	u_e (rule, cube)		

Phase 5 Alternative Pronunciations of Graphemes			
a (hat, what)	e (bed, she)	i (fin, find)	o (hot, so, other)
u (but, unit)	c (cat, cent)	g (got, giant)	ow (cow, blow)
ie (tied, field)	ea (eat, bread)	er (farmer, herb)	ch (chin, school, chef)
y (yes, by, very)	ou (out, shoulder, could, you)		

HERE ARE SOME WORDS WHICH YOUR CHILD MAY FIND TRICKY.

Phase 5 Tricky Words			
oh	their	people	Mr
Mrs	looked	called	asked
could			

TOP TIPS FOR HELPING YOUR CHILD TO READ:

- Allow children time to break down unfamiliar words into units of sound and then encourage children to string these sounds together to create the word.

- Encourage your child to point out any focus phonics when they are used.

- Read through the book more than once to grow confidence.

- Ask simple questions about the text to assess understanding.

- Encourage children to use illustrations as prompts.

This book focuses on /a_e/ and /ai/ and is an Orange level 6 book band.

Can you work out which of these pictures have names with a_e in them?

Answers: crate, cake, cane, plate, snake

Have you ever been to see a play? Plays are not the same as films. The performers are right there!

The performers may sing songs or just speak. Some plays have lots of props, dressing up and makeup. There are all sorts of different plays.

When you have paid for a seat, an usher may help you get to it.

Some sites have seats on different levels.
You can look down on the play from up high.

When the play is about to start, it will go dark. Then, the long drapes will be dragged back and the play will start.

Drapes

An act is a part of the play. Some plays have three acts that make up the start, midway and end parts.

The performers may be far away from the crowd. They paint lots of makeup on so the people in the back can still see it.

They may need new outfits or makeup as the play is still happening.

The performers have to speak up so that all the crowd can hear them. If they do not, people may just hear a faint sound.

In some plays, performers do not need to speak to tell a tale. They may just use their hands and not say a thing.

At the end, all the performers bow as the crowd claps. They wave and wait for the clapping to finish.

You could make a play, too. All you need to do is dress up and have fun!

©2023 **BookLife Publishing Ltd.**
King's Lynn, Norfolk, PE30 4LS, UK

ISBN 978-1-80505-082-7

All rights reserved. Printed in China.
A catalogue record for this book is available from the British Library.

At a Play
Written by Charis Mather
Designed by Isabella Croker

An Introduction to BookLife Readers...

Our Readers have been specifically created in line with the London Institute of Education's approach to book banding and are phonetically decodable and ordered to support each phase of the Letters and Sounds document.

Each book has been created to provide the best possible reading and learning experience. Our aim is to share our love of books with children, providing both emerging readers and prolific page-turners with beautiful books that are guaranteed to provoke interest and learning, regardless of ability.

BOOK BAND GRADED using the Institute of Education's approach to levelling.

PHONETICALLY DECODABLE supporting each phase of Letters and Sounds.

EXERCISES AND QUESTIONS to offer reinforcement and to ascertain comprehension.

CLEAR DESIGN to inspire and provoke engagement, providing the reader with clear visual representations of each non-fiction topic.

AUTHOR INSIGHT:
CHARIS MATHER

Charis Mather is a children's author at BookLife Publishing who has a love for reading and writing. Her studies in linguistics and experiences working with young readers have given her a knack for writing material that suits a range of ages and skill levels. Charis is passionate about producing books that emphasise the fun in reading and is convinced that no matter how much you already know, there is always something new to learn.

PHASE 5 /a_e/ /ai/

This book focuses on /a_e/ and /ai/ and is an Orange level 6 book band.

Image Credits Images are courtesy of Shutterstock.com. With thanks to Getty Images, Thinkstock Photo and iStockphoto. Cover – Ljupco Smokovski, Kilroy79, Rocksweeper. p2–3 – Alex Stemmers, Eky Studio, M. Unal Ozmen, Valentina Razumova, tobibambola, Creatus, Andrey_Kuzmin, VladyslaV Travel photo. p4–5 – Igor Bulgarin, Kozlik. p6–7 – T photography, A_Lesik. p8–9 – Jonas Petrovas. p10–11 – BG Plus2, Nacha Petchdawong. p12–13 – Yuriy Golub, Igor Bulgarin. p14–15 – Robert Kneschke, Kozlik.